In My Life

In My Life

100 New Poems
by
Paul Friedrichs

BURNHAM

PRESS

To my wife Jane and the beautiful life
we have built together.

Contents

I. Nature

Contents

II. Humanity

Contents

III. Love

IV. Serenity

I. Nature

Time to Bloom

Today's the day
your buds are lush
they've captured what your love entrusts
    for desire has traveled in your veins
    and sweetly packaged what remains
from roots well planted in the ground
with sunshine laughing all around

So release your grip
and let it slide
relax your petals to the side
    let your pollen catch the wind
    or little feet of dancing bees
it's time to bloom and let it shout
it's time to let the beauty out.

April at Rocky Point

Amplified voices prelude
before round the bend
comes the longboat regatta,
eights oars flashing
to coach's drill
of catch and let go.
Above the cacophony of birds
an eagle floats by,
scurrying the sparrow
into the brush and
quieting the screech
of the territorial blackbird.
With grass greening
and buds coaxed
by longer days
of healing and growth,
dirt lies hoed in the garden
and all is anticipation.

May

Under crystal sky of bird-busy blue
in bud-pink light and early green
the hummingbird returns to feed
and magnolia petals fall like tears
of happiness for this abundance.
Children swarm the playground
like starlings flocking the trees
as leaves open before our eyes
and grass grows an inch each day
making my heart like a bell
ring farewell to winter
before quieting in the calm
of a languid sunset where
with the fragrance of lilacs
I breathe in contentment
as if life never ends.

Plant Sale

In this season as busy
as bees in the field
I head down the road
past the lilac bushes
and my neighbor's truck
up for bid in his yard
to the community plant sale
outside the art gallery
where the irises hang
already blooming
in anticipation of dirt
under my fingernails
and tomato plants
beginning to flower
I welcome earlier dawns
and lengthening evenings
quite expecting the arrival
of the fireflies
any day now.

Dawn

Cool and pink
like the flesh of fresh-caught fish
    from still waters
I invite you, first light
to open my pores
fill my lungs
flow into my veins
and quicken my heart
with new beginning,
opening the world around me
as if again new.

Sculling the River with My Daughter

There won't be another day quite like this one,
the morning light through the trees just so
and the tide rising to here and now.
Stroke matching stroke we pulled our oars
through the summer-warmed water,
dragonflies darting between us and heron watching
from the shore. As I look back as through a window
at the dock from which we've just come,
water slowly dripping down my long oars,
I press this precious moment to my heart
and it becomes a part of me.

Summer Day

Oh Lord, drink me up,
I am your sweet peach nectar
drawn from succulent sap,
I am your down thistle-seed
floating on air,
your honey bees dancing in yellow pollen
and your crickets filling the field,
I am your trout beneath crystal waters
and your gull drafting high above
as I soak in the sunshine
and blend with this summer day
staying here
in the open palm of your creation
with no better place to be
    until you send the mosquitos
    to remind me all pleasures
    must come to an end.

Bedrock Gardens

First must come hands in dirt
and knees on the ground
before in sun and rain and time
each shoot can rise and
plant line meet sight line
along path meeting path
in sublime meander
among sturdy sculpture built
fire and might from the scraps
of generations
totem silhouette peace flora blade
bugs balancing gem medallions
feather and arrow catching dreams divine
and ferocity in fantail victory
the trickle of water celebrating
below the meditation hut
these elements of serenity
shared with dragonfly and frog
and rabbit and undoubtedly
before sunrise a deer
drinking in the beauty
before I rise to do the same.

Vines

Our journey
fed by sunshine and well-timed rain
is a long vine fingering fences
or the trunk of a weathered tree
seeking footholds of longevity,
each tendril grasping
for a good idea, or companionship,
yearning to entwine a braid of intimacy
yet increasingly distant
from our soil source
and vulnerable to a pruning
by the Great Gardener of life.

I Love That

I love that no matter
how early I arise
the flowers are there to greet me,
no matter how restless my sleep
you are there when I awake,
no matter how far it had to fly
the monarch flirts my garden
and no matter how long they are gone
our children return to stay.

Today I will go about the meadow
walking more slowly and stiffly than I would like
to breathe in the colors of the fall,
absorb the sparkle of the golden grasses in the sunshine,
and allow my heart to follow the thistledown
as it lifts off in the breeze
searching for new ground to seed.

End of Summer

The morning glories and black-eyed Susans
declare as do the goldenrod
and dance of regal monarchs
that summer's end is near—
Yet should the slow drain
of this luscious time
bring regret?
To have awoken in birdsong,
found new blooms daily,
and basked in evening light these many weeks
yet still enjoy the warmth of midday sun
is a gift beyond remorse,
to have surfed the surge of life all round us
calms all anguish---
So we are grateful for each day of earthly march
in this time-bound completion of our lives.

September

Harvest my desire
and place it in the sun
on a warm autumn day
yellowing squash on the vine
apples plump on the tree
peach juice now a memory
like sand between the toes
or the last time we made love
a train whistle in the distance
empty chairs on the porch
a leaf floating in the pool
and geese heading south
as I bask in contentment
of a summer well done.

Rainy Day in Autumn

How quickly
the sun disappears
and the cold rain comes heavy and unforgiving
to steal the remnant warmth
from this autumn day;
now birds flee home for shelter
and small mammals burrow into the ground.
We need this autumn cleansing, this absolution
for our frantic acts of selfishness,
our scurry for favor,
our righteous claims of certitude,
as if the turning of the earth was not
the true rhythm of this universe,
as if any one of us was more
than a blink
in the eye of God.

The Tree

Now in November
you reveal your true self
your garment of foliage
coyly dropped to the floor
while proudly outstretched
in your signature reach
each crook and angle
thinly pasted with snow
still graciously holding
an abandoned bird's nest
you'll have to relinquish
come January gale
you patiently wait
with buds expectant
for the turn of the sun
and the draw of the day.

The Coming of Winter

December rain
washes away the dried remains
of autumn, leaving cold reality
in unkind wind and shallow days,
bare trees in purple light
and birds searching for shelter
as we lay depleted,
huddled in our wollens,
hoping the clouds will part
so we may find the stars.

Snow Day

Here I sit
in my living-room cocoon
snow blowing sideways outside my window
all planning and doing
now waiting and being
paused in this swirling mess
of unfinished love
we call the human condition.
So I go inward
to a grateful interior
thankful to hear the furnace click on
and journey to the kitchen
for a cup of tea
where I feel almost arrived
like seeing the woman
in the red dress and black hat
at the end of the movie
who you can't really touch
except with your desire.

Winter Morning

I wake to quiet and light
in wonderland of new snow,
sparkle in the air, trees laden with beauty
and birds fluttering the feeder.
I am drawn out of doors
with shovel in hand,
an excuse to get some exercise
but mostly to smell the air
and feel the snow-brightened sun on my face.
We are blessed with warmth of shelter,
a full larder, a loving home,
even an overnight visit from the blinking plow.
The paths now clear, I would sit with you
and drink it all in
save for the need
for an emergency trip to the store
for coffee beans.

Ice

Just when you think
all is hibernation
ice comes alive on the river
moving in eddies of tide and current
thick enough at first
for only a gull's perch
or traverse of a light-footed fox
before small pieces meld large sheets that
with the tide
rise in a groan
then settle in snap and creak
releasing pockets of air that
speak to me
as if from a creature below
of life and loss
and time passing in short days
waiting for the next turn,
the next thaw,
the next birth.

The Canyon of Fools (Sedona)

Go deep in the earth of my red rock valley,
my chalky vein of prehistoric life,
climb my steps of genial limestone
and rise like the sun in the desert-blue sky
to dance with the birds in the mountain cedar
or bask like the lizard in the rabbit brush
but do pause to study my shadow-edged cliffs,
for they have stories of deep time to tell
and glimpses of what the future may hold:
like the divergent veins of the Sycamore leaf
your path is of your own choosing.

Dear Sedona

Through your dusty red rocks
your Oak Creek flows,
an artery of rejuvenation past God's
monuments to time and patience,
layered in color as if the rusted blood of ages.
I am sprinkled now with juniper berries,
celebrating cactus flower and jack pine,
ready to take to the air like the mountain jay.

Beach and Sky

Sand wave-ironed flat
Sea sun-sparkle alive
Sky blue-gauzed in high cloud
inviting the gulls to soar
and the boats to bob
in day-licious celebration
far from the bustle
far from the crowds
far from the emptiness
of the peopled kingdom
of worry and woe.

Sanibel Sunset

The majesty of sunset declares me king
and knights this day
in slow-motion pageantry:
Royal terns align in salute,
my pelican subjects head to roost
and arching dolphins home to pod;
the peasant hermit hustles across the sand
while serf shells await their nightly shuffle
by moon-fed tides. What a feat
to celebrate this turning of the earth,
a monument display to trumpet
not just ending
but beginning of another day.

January

Winter breathes the fire of survival
into the belly
while its frigid tongue licks your nose,
fingers and toes. It keeps your socks on
and curls you up in bed
looking for warmth.
Winter is ice on the river,
shoots underground waiting, waiting,
and the cardinal looping from tree to tree
looking for food.
Winter is each day a little longer,
tugging at the sun, begging it to stay.

Winter Beach

Even the longest nights are met by color
on the winter beach at dawn,
pastels that slowly warm
with unexpected generosity
the shuttered homes along its edge,
the frost-rimmed rocks and restless,
hungry gulls. Here the tide
doesn't have the choice of staying
at home in a warm bed
but is compelled to meet the lone dog walker
and the insulated surfer at end of frigid night
as the sun rides with glorious declaration
into the day.
Even in this darkest time of year, every day
is expansive, every day is new.

Driving to the Beach, 5am

Birdsong laughs me eastward
past silent church and fire station and steam
rising like gray smoke from the old schoolhouse furnace
as I head to the beach in the early morning light.
My mind is still in bed whispering to my dreams,
but God's paint brush is moving fast
so my body with coffee beside me is in motion, too
to catch her in the act
painting rose above the purpled light where sky meets sea.
Today is Sunday and it's not yet summer
so I have the roads and the beach to myself,
even the gull churning his wings above the beach is alone.
Why do I do this, why do I want to embrace this new day
as if it were something special, when it is just one
in a row of many, not yet warm enough and still too gray?
Because I have landed here, because I have plopped down
in this world that keeps coming at us
whether we like it or not, so serve it up
and strike the ball
and put it in play.

II. Humanity

Election Day

Day breaks damp
in the morning chill
best to bring an umbrella
and dress in layers
for a long day holding signs
and cups of steaming coffee
as feet stomp to keep toes warm
and familiar names in bold print
bob in dueling colors above wooden sticks
for voters walking the gauntlet
of democracy
seeking admission
to curtained booths of hope
and having cast my humble prayer
I come down the concrete steps
a hurrah for civil discourse in my heart
to find the sun
breaking through the clouds
on this
my favorite day of the year.

Burying Fred

With eighties music playing on the radio
we travel the thruway
in our Sunday best
to the old white church on the green
surprised yet not surprised
that his battle with illness
has come to an end
and his physical presence
reduced to an urn.
Yet in my mind's eye
he's still over my shoulder
reading the paper
or following his stocks on TV
and when I turn
his knowing eyes stare back
like an old horse
surprised by all the fuss.

I am the Lucky One

In your hour of fear
and uncertainty I am called
to your bedside
with many things left undone
and find you, old friend
in a new place
without control of things to come.
So we settle into a new routine
considering loss and grief
and you worry about
my lack of sleep and long hours
in a life of service
to the leaky vessels of humanity
but in holding fast
to the privilege of caring
I am the lucky one.

Bird Talk

You have no idea
how silly you look
building nests on the ground
with cement foundations
So hard to pick up
and follow the seasons
or go and look for
a new berry crop
So sad you can't float
on updrafting air
or fit in a hole
in a hollow tree
So I'll leave you behind
to dig in your gardens
and fly back later
to sample your wares.

Leaving

Like turning a page
or getting on an airplane
you must leave things behind.
Sure, you can go back
and revisit another time,
but it's not the same.
The air is gone, the moment
evaporated, it cannot
be put back in the bottle:
Spent. Vanished. Over.
But to have not been in that
moment, to have not read that
book, to have failed to seek
or have missed that trip
should be the only regret.

Awakening

All I know there is light
and I open my eyes
to the five-petalled flower
of my ceiling fan,
my brain surfacing
as if from a dive
through breakers at the beach,
now cleansed,
the taste of salt in my mouth,
bobbing in the water
alert,
readying myself for the next wave.

The Human Condition

We start out naked
but soon find
without a coat of shiny fur
that wearing textiles is preferred.

Thursday

The penultimate day of the week,
and also a British detective,
you're almost there but not complete,
just tired enough to know the difference.
Not yet worried about packing up
or putting on your best clothes,
a nice night out for dinner or a movie
before the weekend crowds;
you've made your trip to the market
and stocked the fridge,
perhaps finished a load of laundry
and paid the bills.
We live our lives forever on a Thursday,
feeling like we've done a few things
but never really thinking
we've reached the end.

For Umpqua et al.

I sit down to an empty page
and it fills with blood.
Silent now are the screams
and flees in panic
as yet another gun-fueled madman
stoked by unquenched testosterone
has strut his moment on the stage
while an empty handkerchief
floats to the ground.
Where is the warm earth,
where is the open hand,
where are the daffodils of decency?

Aging

Each morning I awake
as if from a bad dream
to find a piece of my body
replaced by a used part---
a rusty back
a stiff shoulder
a weak knee
a newly leaking sinus
an unforgiving toe
or an irate bowel---
while the mind, unchanged
feels fecklessly abandoned
by youth stealing off
as if from a sinking ship
or a failing state
until the shamble which remains
becomes a slow shuffle
down the long corridor
to the coffin-maker's door.

Our Little Town
(written on the occasion of my
40th high school reunion)

The wooden bridge still crosses
the stony brook that talks
and the mountains still hang
like curtains in the distance
but the youth that gather now
outside the pizza parlor
are unfamiliar.
The schoolhouse has shrunk
like the distance I once walked
which I find when I return
and awaken in my past
to re-embrace that young man
who liked hard candies
and baseball in June
and hikes in the woods
always able to come home
to someone else in charge
and dinner on the table
always with a future
with something unimagined
something left undone
now floating untethered
in the blurry-edged crucible
of time.

A Genial Evening

A genial evening with my once younger brother, now
with the passage of time just my brother
as we slip into ease of familiar,
same forehead, same thumbs, same out-toeing gait,
same look to horizon searching phrase or memory,
with fluidity of years
like pouring warm chocolate
not in the same mold
but from the same vessel,
fully understood,
no more competition, just well wishes
to complete each of our lives
as painlessly as possible.

Paris

Your boulevards like ticking hands
of a busy clock,
your river a slate brush-stroke
past islands of history,
your streets cobbled
by the desire of generations
still spilling its youth onto your quais,
your markets teeming
with the colors of life
and your gardens rich
with civilization--
but your churches
are the hidden heart of you,
rich in silence
and still portal
to the eternal now.

La Loire

Under shadows of cathedrals
you wash away the sins of this world
into the mouths of fish
much appreciated by the egrets
who gladly fertilize these fields
for the next generation of diesel-fed humans
locked into global warming
as les vieux chateaux with old wiring
and no central air fade away
among still fecund fields
of rural splendor.

Into the Woods

Entering the forest I go back in time
to past adventures
when small feet and hands
climbed rocks and foraged sticks
among the fallen leaves
or in my youth stole away with my beloved
to a secluded hollow to make love.
In later years I wander paths
of craggy roots alone,
where once I ran now cautiously I walk,
but with each visit I am lost
for a few minutes or an hour in another world
where years become confluent memories
within a melded landscape:
which me will emerge?
A recalled path is now hidden by overgrowth
but I am drawn in
by the wonder of time travel.

Wintery Mix

We arrived at Logan in a wintery mix,
back from the beaches of Florida,
when my wife saw an owl on the ride from the airport,
and wondered what it foretold.
For I have prostate cancer, you know—
though it should work out all right--
just a few more months of feeling awful,
a goal within my sight.

One of our sons is divorced and spent,
just getting his sea legs back;
another's divorcing, his car broken down,
like everything else right now.
His electric heat is too expensive,
so he's selling his house real soon,
but it means we get to play with our grandson,
for as long as our energy lasts.

One daughter is married but not yet pregnant,
another is pregnant but not yet married,
the third, well, her dog is dying,
while our youngest is lonely and too far away,
and yes we sorely miss him.
But we are soon off to the Mexican jungle
to heal beside the Pacific,
our lives stitched together, lovingly,
for whatever the owl might bring.

Retirement

Oh, look!
As I lie on my lounge chair
in the Florida sunshine
a vulture hovers over me.

Every Day We Bathe

Every day we bathe in time
and wash away another layer of ourselves,
those daily moments that settle like dust on our stories,
like the dust I wipe from the frames
of old pictures on my shelves
where younger versions of ourselves
stare back as if distant relatives,
amusingly recognizable yet
no longer us,
like remembering a field that is now a house,
a path that is now overgrown,
or a beach that has washed away.

Passover (2018)

They march because a boy came in their school
and gunned them down.
They don't want it to happen again,
don't want other families to suffer,
don't want to live under the shadow of a gun--
    Pass over my pain, pass over my anger,
    pass over my fear.
She fights cancer that has spread
to her liver and her brain. Now she's weak
with trouble thinking and walking,
but still talks of love
for this life and those around her--
    Pass over my pain, pass over my anger,
    pass over my fear.
It was a stupid accident
but now in a coma on a machine
he breathes through broken bones and injured brain:
Will he lose a leg or lose it all?
    Pass over my pain, pass over my anger,
    pass over my fear.
Aging is slow but relentless,
every year I forfeit range and drive,
and as others I know fall ill around me
every night I leave some blood upon my door--
    Pass over my pain, pass over my anger,
    pass over my fear.

Radiation

Into the lion's mouth I go
through the bunker's artificial light
and the tastefully done waiting room
to the jaws of the big machine
where I must lay still in the clench
of its pin-point teeth
holding the blue ring of hope*
and counting my two minute buzz
while green laser-light dances
on the ceiling above
before I am let go, tossed
and toyed with,
invited to return and play
another day.

*[a rubber ring patients may hold during treatment to keep their arms
out of the radiation field.]

Gettysburg

Morning breaks grey on the battlefield
as we venture forth to taste the waters of history,
fog hanging as if from campfires along the ridge
in the hush of this open-air cathedral.
How rude to drive a car along this somber expanse
of mortal endeavor, best to walk or ride a horse,
though a bicycle will do
following the dust of a hundred thousand men marching,
cannon, cannon everywhere
as ghosts two rows thick step into the grassy fields
exhorting onward, sword held high,
stepping over ball-shattered bodies one imagines
gloves and satchels and epaulets still layered on the ground.
Then the quiet of night, spring peepers
estimating the groans of fallen men
before in rosy dawn the smell again of campfires
and bacon grease filling the air with almost—
almost done, almost survived, almost won.

Shadowland

In the gray hours of the night
burdened by awakenings
stiff of body and of soul
    the tissue's in the jar
Counting months from there to here
wondering what my fate will be
holidays are poignant now
    the tissue's in the jar
Lying on the stretcher stripped
watching numbers rise and fall
finished treatment, cancer gone?
    waiting for the dawn
Walking in company, walking alone
reaching out to hold your hand
living life in shadowland
    the tissue's in the jar.

[Biopsy and surgical tissue specimens are placed in a jar of formalin to
preserve for laboratory diagnosis.]

Things Just Happen

Do you remember, Alicia, that night we learned
that sometimes things just happen—
like the girl, just five, who dropped her doll
crossing the road with her parents and
just as the light turned green
for cars hurtling down the avenue
darted back to collect it
and caught big-eyed in their fold
was flung to the curb just steps
from our Emergency Room,
where her ruptured spleen and fractured liver
and torn vessels were too far gone
to save despite skilled surgeons' hands, and us
suctioning blood from the table, coaxing the fluids
to bring back her heart, bring back her smile
to greet her father pacing the hallway,
hoping against hope,
feeling her slip away,
and how we held each other after,
interns in the baptism of failure,
knowing the fragility of life.

Left Standing

A big wind came last night
and took down the spread oak
which stood so proudly along the riverbank,
just took it down while its neighbors stood rooted,
a tangle of broken limbs and folded branches
as if its sixty-five years meant nothing
to the breath of God.
And you left us, too,
one might say in your prime,
the same age as the tree,
your spread of goodness like
broad branches reaching out
in the care of others, providing
nesting shelter and comforting shade
beneath your generous canopy.
And I am left standing,
wondering what happened,
wondering where the time went,
feeling the heaviness of my own branches,
the loneliness without you,
the nakedness of my own resolve,
a formerly stalwart member
of a thinning forest.

Persistence

When I face an unwieldy task,
an uphill climb, an unbending partisan
I often count to myself.
When I fear I don't have the strength,
the will, the patience, I just count
to ten, then fifty, or a hundred or a thousand
until I find I can do it after all.
Or I read history, to remind myself
how power and justice have shifted
over the centuries back towards the disenfranchised.
I matter
You matter
We matter
Everyone matters.
They say, those who study it,
that rescuers act on impulse.
They rush without thinking to save the family
trapped by fire, the woman swept away
by wild water, the man still breathing
under an avalanche.
The Samaritan doesn't ask what language they speak,
or the color of their skin,
or how they came here,
does not act on a legacy of jealousy or spite,
just recognizes the value of another human being
held lovingly, the way each innocent child
is welcomed into this world.

III. Love

Generosity

I give to you,
from my will and from my body,
as in an act of birth
and place you in the foreground
of my desire.
The world turns, and I give it to you,
the sun rises, and I give it to you,
milk and honey flow, and I pour them
for you.
May your vibrancy sprout
from the humus of my own spent life,
and may you launch on powerful strokes
of eagle's wings.

The Rejoining

Throw me a lifeline,
that forgotten part of you
dropped overboard
in the aft-spent sea;
Realize now
that you have missed me,
that broken part
you tried doing without.
Though not at my best
in my rusted state,
pull me on deck
to rejoin the crew;
Learn what you can
from the places you've been,
be a good friend
to your old self, too.

Broken

Depart the land of broken toys,
of wounded little girls and boys,
shackled by that nagging voice
of insufficiency.
Scared, alone and often mute
you've traveled a forbidding route,
it's time to show you're ready now
for possibility.
Let go and touch the face of joy,
resolve to truly love yourself
the beauty of the human face
the promise of the human race.

Say Yes

Sing, sing for a life well lived
a rainbow of pleasures
a basketful of woe,
an intimate gift
down a garden path
which we would have missed
if we hadn't said 'go'
So say Yes to the heartache
say Yes to the pain
say Yes to adventure and
discover the gain,
stoke the fire while the flame
is high in its hearth
soon enough will come embers
and a time to depart.

In Search of Beauty

In search of beauty
I watch my wife
enter the room to rearrange
the flowers she's just picked
in our garden,
blessed with morning light,
elegant in all her years,
ripe with the day.
The windows lay open
to the late September sun
where tomatoes still ripen on the vine
and life still forages in the field
not yet mowed.
At this moment, before breakfast,
all life is in the palm of my hand,
and like the birds chattering in the hedges
I pay no mind to the coming chill
of autumn nights.

Remembrance

Sometimes you must see
your grandchildren at play
to remember your best self,
inquisitive and carefree,
adventurous and trusting,
when everything was sunshine and light.
Wisdom isn't always
passed from old to young,
but flows all ways
from spirit to vessel.

The Inner Sanctum

Now we enter new territory,
treading with the intimacy of light touch,
unshackled by cancer treatment
from raw libido and old formulas,
encountering tears of bewilderment
with nothing to prove
and nowhere to go
except deeper
into a new language of love.

The Miracles of My Life

Healing, growing,
waking up each day.
My children, our children,
baby birds at play.
Sunshine, thunderstorms,
the greening of the field,
rising bread, tasty wine,
lovingly made meals.
Touching base by telephone
with loved ones far away,
finding open blossoms
and inviting them to stay.
Morning light, daydreams,
twinkle of a star,
flashing aspiration
of a firefly in a jar.

My Desire

What do I desire most?
Is it a peaceful walk on the beach
with you, hand in hand,
or restful slumber
in sweet-smelling sheets?
Is it a timeless life of exploration
and discovery,
or just one moment when our souls touch?
Is it the ability to affect change?
Is it joy and laughter, or gentle caress
in the evening after a hard fought day?
Is it World Peace? No,
I simply desire
that all persons on this earth
may experience the feeling
of being loved.

What is Hidden

lavender under the snow
fish under the ice
crocuses in the garden
answers to the voice of love.

Open House

My heart is an open house,
sliders left open to let the breeze in,
everything invited
and everything welcomed
yet not everything can stay,
as I need to close the door at night
and sleep in a warm bed
with my beloved.

Climaxed

Floating away on a cloud
the spent canister of a rocket shell
with vanishing legs
and sinking lids
softening breath
and teeth unclenched
off to sleep I go snoring.

Fantasy Footsies

Geez, is that a sparkle in your eyes,
a coming smile
as I inch towards you
heart-leaning,
ready for warm touch?
Mistletoeing my inhibition
I first with cool fingers take
your hands but
warmed by the heat of desire
you answer with your lips
to say, open-mouthed,
I will.

From a Distance

I see you from a distance
in a pink straw hat
your skin soft in the summer sun
and your sweet smell rising with the hollyhocks
or at least I imagine it's you
across the field
in conversation with friends
wishing it were me
you were smiling to
and planning to take
away to your bed
and hold to your breast
my weary soul.

Missed Communication

Word came on the internet
Wireless-ether-wi-fi
without face, inflection, or context--
What were you thinking?
Don't you know how I feel?
So we entered the Shostakovich symphony
of human emotion
and I pulled up a chair
to begin tuning the static
into usable wavelengths of genuine
conversation.

Receiving

My heart is the orange Koi
in the lily pond
filled by gentle rain.

Christmas

Tradition opens our hearts
like a plow turns warm earth
to lie steaming in the evening chill
as we stand gathered round our kin
open-palmed in our imperfection
following as if by braille the old script
which brings us strings of holiday light
and bowls of holiday cheer
to fight the darkness of the season
and invites us to sprawl under the tree
shredding paper and sorting ribbon
into piles that soon become yesterday
as we quietly fold away
another year of forgiveness.

Change

Heavy snowfall came and overnight
branches of the big pine
snapped under their weight,
leaving a new silhouette
against the morning sky.
Something to get used to
like a pair of new shoes
or new neighbors whose names
you might remember when awakening
in a season somehow misremembered
but soon grow accustomed to
like yesterday becoming today
or your wife's face slowly changing
as you live together
into the evolving habit of now.

Peaches

When I was a boy
my favorite food was peaches,
sun-warmed and soft,
each bite with slurp reflexed
to catch its run of sweetness.
Round and full
like a deep embrace,
you took me to a place of all things,
all needs met
in momentary completeness.
Now as I pull you free
from your pregnantly-bent branch,
find your soft fur
and bite into your pliant flesh
I am a boy once more.

The Love that Speaks to Everything

I am the daughter that God searches when He's lonely,
I am the wind that touches all the grasses of the field,
I am the turning of the earth upon its axis
and the tears a mother cries for her lost child.
I am the dust trod by feet of homeless masses
dispossessed by evil masters gone to war,
and their warm embrace into a land of plenty
by a people grateful for the things they have.
I am the timeless flow of energy between all things,
the dancing particles announcing each and every atom,
I am the blanket that covers all the night,
I am the potential for all things,
the breath of God,
the love that speaks to everything.

Book Club

Considered, thoughtful, the men drift in
and the circle fills,
greeting and well-wishing
as bottle tops snap
and wine corks pop,
entering a fold of genuine respect
for the sheen worn by each of us
from decades of trying,
building and caring and doing.
The books are dropped on the table or floor
and the torch passed round.
Each knows the work of being
a partner, a parent, a citizen
of this crazy world,
and though we stand to a man
each knows the death of a father
or the father of a friend.
Chiding and teasing and disagreement
weave into our fabric, but it is love
that binds us together.

Rejoice

The magnolia blossoms gladly open
in the abundant sunshine
on this warm spring day
and offer their beauty to the world.

Turning my face towards the sun
I've decided
is the first step towards self love
which is the first step towards generosity.

On the Beach

I celebrate this sun-strewn morning
on the beach, each cresting wave
exhaled as passing time,
each bird call acclamation of the new.
The setting moon is gone, the rosy hue
of dawn arisen and aloft
leaving the sanderlings and willets and ruddy
turnstone
scouring for tidal treasures,
and my eyes drawn down to find the shells.

I cannot hold us here forever;
I do not know if I would want to.
Our lives will end as will this season,
but in the coming of what's next I know
I will meet you there.

The Gift

The two halves of sorrow parted
and there you stood, embroidered in godfullness,
open, seeking, listening, offering,
you did not settle easily
but stayed curious to my desires,
guarding your intimacy while slowly opening
your heart, elegant and poised
wearing carefully your Degas dancer's body
you were open to explore marriage
in an Ecuadorian cloud forest
two-stepping our meld before full-throttle
holding me through my hour of need,
giving always giving the gift
of you to me.
Stumbling, I found you, found you
over my obstinacy and am blessed
for it. Reading me without words
you guide me to the voice of love.

01/01/2019

New Year, New day
The furnace is working
and I am alive, alive!
I won't worry about money,
I will rise with the sun, I will go and smell the ocean.
A few more weeks of socks in bed
and then south for toes in the sand
and bicycling and shuffleboard.
The dolphins and manatees are calling,
the big brown pelicans and shorebirds
and hopefully the black skimmers, too
with fresh-squeezed oranges
juicing my shoreline poetry
It's time, It's time to hold your hand
and walk off into the sunset.

IV. Serenity

Righting Things

After the storm, it is time to walk the land
and set things right again.
Small dead branches can winter in place
but limbs need dragging
into the brush at the edge of the field,
White Buffalo Calf Woman needs righting
onto her wrought-iron pedestal,
and the bench overlooking the pier
whose dock now sits on blocks behind the garage
must be set upright
should a sunny day come along
to welcome a visitor.
The canoe must be flipped
to empty its cargo of rain water
and put in the shed for winter,
joined by the deck chairs retrieved
from the brambles where
they've sailed in the wind.
Everything has weathered another notch,
but lacking vanity will return
for re-use in the spring, when surrounded
by bright greens and flower blossoms
they will be beautiful once more.

Surrender

Surrender to the radiance of God.
There is little needing proof
other than that we can love.
There is no first in line to receive the sunrise,
there is no shortage of earth or air,
just lack of imagination
with what to do with it.
While we cannot defeat death,
there is no shortage of eternity,
just quality of our imprint upon it.
May I leave mine gently
and kindly and lovingly.
May I sing joyfully like
birds flocking to the trees.

Autumn Kitchen

Onions and apples cook on the stove
soon to be joined by squash
in harvest symphony
as the low light drifts into dusk
and the golden glow of the field
becomes the brown of autumn night.
My love passes in and out,
chopping and dicing
before the soup is set to stew
and we settle down for a glass of sherry.
What comfort warmth is,
the draw of roasting chicken
and softening lentils
in this time of year when
a taste for cranberries tickles my palate,
I search for my slippers again,
and a hot beverage and blanket
under a lamp
become a part
of the evening ritual.

December Crossing to Martha's Vineyard

Leave all things behind, all failure, all fatigue
and embrace the gray light of a wintering sea
by boarding a cold boat bound for the far light
of this beckoning island's now skeletal towns

Find shuttered stores and summer homes
whose colors have drained back into the sea
taking with them the bustle that no longer matters
for regardless the season, this island breathes on

The salt air re-freshens, the silence revives you,
and walking along the now private beaches
your heart still listens to the sounds worth attending:
the waves on the shore and your feet on the sand.

Dawn II

A hint of light appears in the east
to draw me from bed
to let in the day
as the gentlest of pink
marks a wisp of cloud
in the bluing sky.
Soon mist marks the river
whose edges appear, then sharpen
before the horizon becomes
a blaze of fiery orange.
From the constant hum of crickets
stir bird calls
as they work the room
with claims on the new day.
Clouds fade to purple, then gray
and as yellow assumes the horizon
the insect world revives
in the newly discovered colors of the field.

Vermont Lessons

Choose your valley and settle in,
then stick around.
There's another one next door
if you need the change, but
you'll bring the same problems with you.
The earth loves you, the apples need picking,
and the deer expect company.
The seasons will come and go
and pay you no mind.
The mountains will change color too, but
keep their shape.
Only you will look different
year to year.

Sunset

Raking up the colors of the day
I gather memories in my grasp
like handfuls of fallen petals
bound to slip through my fingers
in the draw of time.

Now sound quiets
into the simple songs of evening
like crickets, or the waves
or the running of a faucet,

while the hard-won calm of the day
is held in a moment of repose
before sleep summons
and all is flushed
in the backwash of the night

and I rise again
from the confusion of my dreams
to rewrite by habit
another day.

Morning Walk on Under Mountain Road

Leaving town in the early morning light
I pass the hum of an air conditioner,
gurgle of a backyard fountain and hiss of a sprinkler
before crickets join the hush of my rubber soles
along the country road.
This world is all mine now,
save for the stare of long-faced horses
from their misty field and the caw-caw-caw
of jockeying crows in the treetops.
Light ebbs higher, layering the hilltops
and mottling leaves until finally
in an explosion of yellows and greens
the sun appears.
How grateful I am to have this harvest time
after busy days of constant obligation,
gardening now the inside rows of my being,
hoeing my true nature,
cultivating my foremost self.

Sanibel Beachcombing at Dawn

Like Christmas morning I awaken
to go and find what the sea
has left me in the night,
straining in the rosy light
to tease shapes and colors,
sorting old from new debris
along the tide line in the sand.
As if in search of lost innocence
I make time for no other task
than this proper meeting of a new day.
If only life were so simple
as rising each day to collect
the light, then home
for coffee and a rest,
leaving time for warming sand
to invite me back with book and towel
to complete the requirements
of the day.

Findings

I am not a fisherman, but I think I know
the idea: Put yourself out there
like a bob on the line,
and give it time.
When I search for shells,
I put myself out there,
walk the beach with the tide
and give it time to make the find,
knowing for sure it will come.
The same is true for life in general,
you must know when
to search, when to rest,
when to trust in fate
and put yourself out there.
You can't just come for ten minutes
and leave. But if you walk
the beach enough, the dolphins will come;
if you rise early enough,
the black skimmers will greet you;
if you go out each day, you'll sometimes
own the beach alone;
if you look long enough, that shell
will rise to meet you.

Cancer Lessons

It's all part of the journey.
Don't make it your life's work.
Define yourself in other ways.
Love your body more, not less.
It's all just damn inconvenience.
All of life is death's waiting room,
but this day is mine.
This day is mine.

Acceptance

Slow down.
Rest.
Your body can't keep up with you.
Like an old engine, it needs reprieve
from full-throttle revolution.
It can give you more
if you love it, if you pace it,
if you rest it on hot days.
There are new models
that will pass you on the highway,
but that is not the point.
Let grace decide when your time
to stop has come.

Yoga in a Beautiful Garden

Through a curtain of grief I enter the garden
for afternoon yoga under crystalline skies
and unroll my mat in this natural beauty
with blossoms and insects now at my side.
I am just off the phone with my loving sister
who's caught in depression and counting her losses,
soon I will witness my dear widowed friend
sweep out her home with her whole world in boxes,
but I have this time to breathe in the day
and feel the stretch of this mortal body,
smell the grass and count the dragonflies,
follow the sun and be caught in its sway.
While across the world the bodies collect
from an Italian earthquake or a Syrian bomb,
I have the sound of the drop of an acorn,
the flight of a bee and the breeze through the leaves;
while high above comes the trail of a jet plane
carrying hundreds of people with their luggage of hope,
I am here in this heavenly garden
breathing mind into body and heart into soul.

Silence

After the crying is done,
the mutterings and eulogies said,
the bags unpacked and the dress clothes hung away
comes a rich silence
which may become a threshold
to the realm of peace.
How can you battle the fact
of a body stone cold and lifeless
or a marriage finished long ago?
Enter now this time of quiet,
of reflection, sit back
and let acceptance spill a rainbow over you:
for what is the frontier, if not
the resilience of the human heart?

Lenox

Treetops, steeple tops
every shade of green,
restaurants, cute shops
yoga on the lawn,
warm breeze, picnic basket
music in the air,
stately houses, antique inns
invitation everywhere.
Walking up the hills and down
past the mansions out of town,
on the road to Lee and Stockbridge
verdant fields and wooded rock ridge,
relaxing shade in summertime
vibrant colors in the fall,
gentle snows in wintertime
welcome seasons all.

OBX

Bent over sand at sunrise
to finger a beckoning shell
this world is all mine and waves
sounding their song of time

Perched on the edge of schedule and task
I now own only my footsteps,
receiving the wind and breathing the surf
that laps against the driftwood

Soon to be joined by the rising sun,
the swooping gulls and a squadron of pelicans,
I wistfully watch for a pod of dolphins
to consecrate the day.

Vacances

Like a line of Degas dancers
windmills in the Val de Loire
pose on the hilltop
in the speckled sunshine
of a Monet blue spring day,
moving here and there
with outstretched arms,
bowing to time
under eloquent clouds
in a march of centuries
among chateaux and rivers
flowing through history,
our car hurtling towards Paris
and a plane hurtling towards home,
but our hearts remaining always
in the timeless gardens of France.

Imperfection

This year I went out
after the storm
in my scarred, imperfect body
to walk amongst the spent, broken shells
on the beach.
Other years I'd find a perfect shell,
radiant, proud, waiting for me
in the blend of two worlds where sea meets shore.
This year I must settle for the battered,
the worn, the imperfect shells that scatter the sand
clinging to the wet in forlorn abandonment.
This year, I gratefully finger
the ragged and pocked fans
that stumble my way.
How humbly I accept my new station,
glad to be here on the beach again,
glad to be in my unique self.

Time

What power there is awakening among mountains
three-hundred million years old,
layered in pleistocene, holocene, paleozoic,
raised from a seabed two miles
into the Arizona sky.
What is time here?
Not a single rotation around this axis or this sun,
certainly not folding laundry or a trip to the market,
not one mammalian lifetime or even a trip to Mars.
Sit for a while among the antelope bones
here in the desert
and think on who you are.

On the Rim of the Grand Canyon

Speak to me, rock temples,
whisper in the wind
of your timelessness,
or show me in your weathered face
tinted with desert varnish
that age becomes beauty
and I should fear not
my fleeting presence here,
as a grain of sand doubts not
its contribution to
this splendid universe.

In Meditation

Imagination carries me
through the walls that fear has wrought,
breathing deeply, breathing free,
aware beyond awareness sought,
while intellect is caught in time,
emotion lets me wander,
releasing me from here and now
to join a state of wonder
and touch the faces of my past,
hold the place between the lines,
listen to essential truths,
find the heartland that is mine,
   Home to my desire,
   Home to the divine.

The Cemetery

Every day I cycle through the cemetery,
a steady pace, respectful,
past the clipped grass, fresh flags and sometimes
new flowers,
gravestones well groomed in their antiquity,
and find myself alone
save for the occasional gravedigger leaning on his spade
or resting in the shade
after opening a new portal in the earth.
How much these people have left behind
for me to now enjoy:
grandchildren, and picnics,
the tall pines and shade of broad maples,
the sunlit sky and birds in it, the squirrels and
chipmunks scurrying for acorns,
the butter- and dragonflies, caterpillars and even
beetles in the garden.
Through all this I sail, enjoying my legs as they circle
the pedals,
my breath moving in and out so easily,
blessed to be passing through another bountiful day.

Haramara Retreat

Unto myself
I fold this used body

For sustenance
I shall be still

Give allowance
for rejuvenation

and Make plans
for a new day to come

Stretch out
in this natural beauty

Come awake
to the call of birds

Say yes
to love's intention

and Embrace
this vibrant life.

Grieve

My old friend Grieve
bulldozed in to crumple the day
like a sucker punch you know you'll get over
but boy does it ache in the belly,
and moving from curled up in bed
to the outer world and back again
doesn't help.
The slow seep of air from spirit
into a space where no breathing is allowed,
just waiting
just waiting for the air to stir
and the ripple of a new breeze.

Listening

Angel in the treetops, talk to me:
share your wisdom and your purity.
You can fly naked and unburdened
from treetop to treetop,
darting like the swallow from perch to perch,
knowing your direction in alms
and good deeds.
Let me share the joy of giving,
attending, and listening:
let me feel the presence of God.

Tell me the truth about my mortality:
Is it a boundless ocean that I will be set free upon
to drift in the sun and rain, the night and day,
rocked by gentle waves in timeless rest,
with no external needs?
Let me be quiet in my own thoughts, alive with
memories of my loves, guarded by a special angel
that is my own true self.

*Paul Friedrichs is a family doctor
and lives with his family in Exeter, NH*